THE WRITER'S ANNUAL
PLANNER

MY WRITING PROJECTS FOR THIS YEAR

*When I schedule things, I make
small steps towards my dreams.*

First published by Rising Spirit; Where Great Ideas Grow
in 2023, Perth, WA, Australia

This edition published in 2023
Copyright ©2023 Alyssa Curtayne

The right of Alyssa Curtayne to be identified as author of this work has been asserted in accordance with the Copyright, Designs and Patents Act 1988.

This publication is copyright. Apart from any use as permitted under the Copyright Act 1968, no part may be reproduced by any process without prior permission from the publisher/author.

www.alyssacurtayne.com

THE WRITER'S ANNUAL
PLANNER

MY WRITING PROJECTS FOR THIS YEAR

compiled by Alyssa Curtayne

Welcome

This is your opportunity to take that writing dream and make it happen.

Scheduling, even if you don't meet the deadlines, can help you to make steps towards completing writing projects, both big and small.

My name is Alyssa Curtayne and I am a writer, researcher, storyteller, and publisher from Perth, Western Australia.

I floundered around for many years with my writing because I never really had a programme or plan. It is my intention for this planner is to share my planning process with you that can provide some strategies to make your writing dreams a reality.

For many writers when we start, we have ideas, hundreds of them! But unless we prioritise each project and have a system of organising our thoughts, we can be stuck in procrastination and overwhelm.

I've designed this planner with the creative, ideas-rich writer in mind.

We start with some BIG dreaming - put your biggest dreams into it! Then we break it down into years, months, weeks, and days, so by the end of the year, you will have made progress toward your finished projects.

I hope this planner helps you to stay motivated and enthused, even in those dark moments of the process.

Happy writing!

~Alyssa

Big Dreams

DREAMS FOR THIS YEAR

_____
_____
_____
_____
_____
_____
_____
_____

DREAMS FOR NEXT YEAR

_____
_____
_____
_____
_____
_____
_____
_____

FIVE YEAR DREAMS

_____
_____
_____
_____
_____
_____
_____

MY BIG, CRAZY DREAMS

This year's Major Project 1

GOAL

Break down your goal into 3 simple targets:

| Target 1 | Target 2 | Target 3 |

Action Steps: Action Steps: Action Steps:

Major Project 2

GOAL

Break down your goal into 3 simple targets:

Target 1

Target 2

Target 3

Action Steps:

Action Steps:

Action Steps:

Minor Project 1

GOAL

Break down your goal into 3 simple targets:

Target 1   Target 2   Target 3

Action Steps: Action Steps: Action Steps:

_____   _____   _____

_____   _____   _____

_____   _____   _____

_____   _____   _____

Minor Project 2

GOAL

Break down your goal into 3 simple targets:

Target 1   Target 2   Target 3

Action Steps: Action Steps: Action Steps:

Minor Project 3

GOAL

Break down your goal into 3 simple targets:

Target 1

Target 2

Target 3

Action Steps:

Action Steps:

Action Steps:

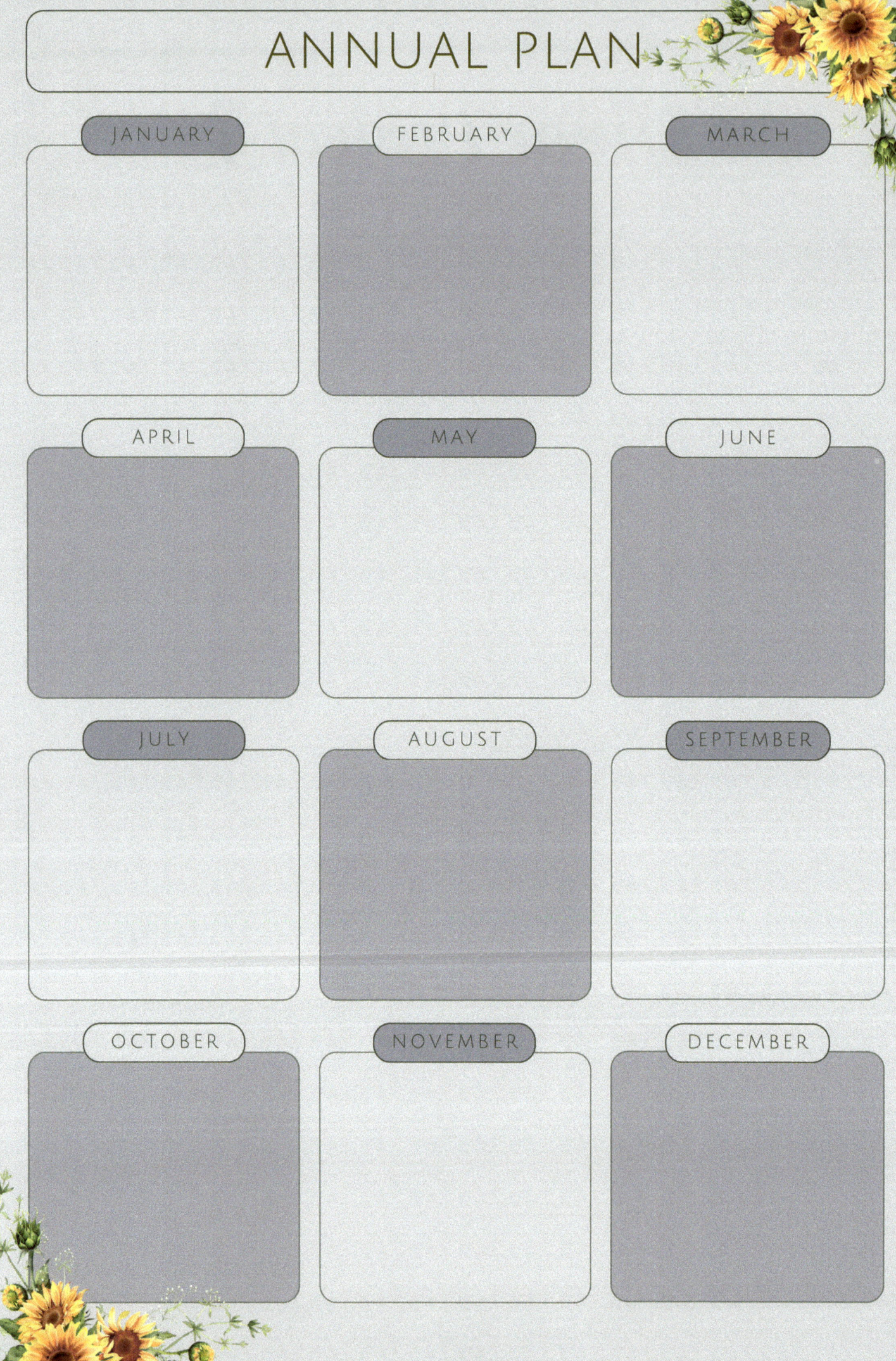

January

MUST DO:

BE NICE IF:

January

1	2	3	4	5	6	7
8	9	10	11	12	13	14
15	16	17	18	19	20	21
22	23	24	25	26	27	28
29	30	31				

Writing Priorities
- ○
- ○
- ○
- ○
- ○
- ○

Marketing
- ●
- ●
- ●
- ●
- ●

Editing Priorities
- ○
- ○
- ○
- ○
- ○
- ○

Other
_____
_____
_____
_____
_____
_____
_____

GOALS THIS WEEK

MONDAY

TUESDAY

WEDNESDAY

THURSDAY

FRIDAY

SATURDAY

SUNDAY

GOALS THIS WEEK

MONDAY

TUESDAY

WEDNESDAY

THURSDAY

FRIDAY

SATURDAY

SUNDAY

GOALS THIS WEEK

MONDAY

TUESDAY

WEDNESDAY

THURSDAY

FRIDAY

SATURDAY

SUNDAY

GOALS THIS WEEK

- MONDAY
- TUESDAY
- WEDNESDAY
- THURSDAY
- FRIDAY
- SATURDAY
- SUNDAY

GOALS THIS WEEK

MONDAY

TUESDAY

WEDNESDAY

THURSDAY

FRIDAY

SATURDAY

SUNDAY

'Shiny' ideas this month

IDEA 1:

IDEA 2:

IDEA 3:

IDEA 4:

MONTHLY CHECK-IN

WHAT I ACHIEVED THIS MONTH

WEEK 1	WEEK 2	WEEK 3	WEEK 4

WEEK 5

STEPS TOWARDS GOALS

Notes

February

MUST DO:

BE NICE IF:

February

1	2	3	4	5	6	7
8	9	10	11	12	13	14
15	16	17	18	19	20	21
22	23	24	25	26	27	28
29						

Writing Priorities
- ○
- ○
- ○
- ○
- ○
- ○

Marketing
- ●
- ●
- ●
- ●
- ●

Editing Priorities
- ○
- ○
- ○
- ○
- ○
- ○

Other
_____
_____
_____
_____
_____
_____
_____

GOALS THIS WEEK

- MONDAY -

- TUESDAY -

- WEDNESDAY -

- THURSDAY -

- FRIDAY -

- SATURDAY -

- SUNDAY -

GOALS THIS WEEK

MONDAY

TUESDAY

WEDNESDAY

THURSDAY

FRIDAY

SATURDAY

SUNDAY

GOALS THIS WEEK

MONDAY

TUESDAY

WEDNESDAY

THURSDAY

FRIDAY

SATURDAY

SUNDAY

GOALS THIS WEEK

- MONDAY
- TUESDAY
- WEDNESDAY
- THURSDAY
- FRIDAY
- SATURDAY
- SUNDAY

'Shiny' ideas this month

IDEA 1:

IDEA 2:

IDEA 3:

IDEA 4:

MONTHLY CHECK-IN

WHAT I ACHIEVED THIS MONTH

WEEK 1	WEEK 2	WEEK 3	WEEK 4

WEEK 5

STEPS TOWARDS GOALS

Notes:

March

MUST DO:

BE NICE IF:

March

1	2	3	4	5	6	7
8	9	10	11	12	13	14
15	16	17	18	19	20	21
22	23	24	25	26	27	28
29	30	31				

Writing Priorities
- ○
- ○
- ○
- ○
- ○
- ○
- ○

Editing Priorities
- ○
- ○
- ○
- ○
- ○
- ○
- ○

Marketing
- ●
- ●
- ●
- ●
- ●

Other
_____
_____
_____
_____
_____
_____
_____

GOALS THIS WEEK

- MONDAY
- TUESDAY
- WEDNESDAY
- THURSDAY
- FRIDAY
- SATURDAY
- SUNDAY

GOALS THIS WEEK

MONDAY

TUESDAY

WEDNESDAY

THURSDAY

FRIDAY

SATURDAY

SUNDAY

GOALS THIS WEEK

MONDAY

TUESDAY

WEDNESDAY

THURSDAY

FRIDAY

SATURDAY

SUNDAY

GOALS THIS WEEK

- MONDAY
- TUESDAY
- WEDNESDAY
- THURSDAY
- FRIDAY
- SATURDAY
- SUNDAY

GOALS THIS WEEK

- MONDAY -

- TUESDAY -

- WEDNESDAY -

- THURSDAY -

- FRIDAY -

- SATURDAY -

- SUNDAY -

'Shiny' ideas this month

IDEA 1:

IDEA 2:

IDEA 3:

IDEA 4:

MONTHLY CHECK-IN

WHAT I ACHIEVED THIS MONTH

WEEK 1	WEEK 2	WEEK 3	WEEK 4

WEEK 5

STEPS TOWARDS GOALS

Notes: _____
_____
_____
_____

April

MUST DO:

BE NICE IF:

April

1	2	3	4	5	6	7
8	9	10	11	12	13	14
15	16	17	18	19	20	21
22	23	24	25	26	27	28
29	30					

Writing Priorities
- ○
- ○
- ○
- ○
- ○
- ○

Marketing
- ●
- ●
- ●
- ●
- ●

Editing Priorities
- ○
- ○
- ○
- ○
- ○
- ○

Other
_____
_____
_____
_____
_____
_____
_____

GOALS THIS WEEK

MONDAY

TUESDAY

WEDNESDAY

THURSDAY

FRIDAY

SATURDAY

SUNDAY

GOALS THIS WEEK

MONDAY

TUESDAY

WEDNESDAY

THURSDAY

FRIDAY

SATURDAY

SUNDAY

GOALS THIS WEEK

MONDAY

TUESDAY

WEDNESDAY

THURSDAY

FRIDAY

SATURDAY

SUNDAY

GOALS THIS WEEK

- MONDAY
- TUESDAY
- WEDNESDAY
- THURSDAY
- FRIDAY
- SATURDAY
- SUNDAY

GOALS THIS WEEK

— MONDAY —

— TUESDAY —

— WEDNESDAY —

— THURSDAY —

— FRIDAY —

— SATURDAY —

— SUNDAY —

'Shiny' ideas this month

IDEA 1:

IDEA 2:

IDEA 3:

IDEA 4:

MONTHLY CHECK-IN

WHAT I ACHIEVED THIS MONTH

WEEK 1	WEEK 2	WEEK 3	WEEK 4

WEEK 5

STEPS TOWARDS GOALS

Notes:
_____
_____
_____
_____

May

MUST DO:

BE NICE IF:

May

1	2	3	4	5	6	7
8	9	10	11	12	13	14
15	16	17	18	19	20	21
22	23	24	25	26	27	28
29	30	31				

Writing Priorities
- ○
- ○
- ○
- ○
- ○
- ○

Marketing
- ●
- ●
- ●
- ●
- ●

Editing Priorities
- ○
- ○
- ○
- ○
- ○
- ○

Other
_____
_____
_____
_____
_____
_____
_____

GOALS THIS WEEK

MONDAY

TUESDAY

WEDNESDAY

THURSDAY

FRIDAY

SATURDAY

SUNDAY

GOALS THIS WEEK

MONDAY

TUESDAY

WEDNESDAY

THURSDAY

FRIDAY

SATURDAY

SUNDAY

GOALS THIS WEEK

MONDAY

TUESDAY

WEDNESDAY

THURSDAY

FRIDAY

SATURDAY

SUNDAY

GOALS THIS WEEK

MONDAY

TUESDAY

WEDNESDAY

THURSDAY

FRIDAY

SATURDAY

SUNDAY

GOALS THIS WEEK

MONDAY

TUESDAY

WEDNESDAY

THURSDAY

FRIDAY

SATURDAY

SUNDAY

'Shiny' ideas this month

IDEA 1:

IDEA 2:

IDEA 3:

IDEA 4:

MONTHLY CHECK-IN

WHAT I ACHIEVED THIS MONTH

WEEK 1	WEEK 2	WEEK 3	WEEK 4

WEEK 5

STEPS TOWARDS GOALS

Notes:
_____
_____
_____
_____

June

MUST DO:

BE NICE IF:

June

1	2	3	4	5	6	7
8	9	10	11	12	13	14
15	16	17	18	19	20	21
22	23	24	25	26	27	28
29	30	31				

Writing Priorities
- ○
- ○
- ○
- ○
- ○
- ○

Marketing
- ●
- ●
- ●
- ●
- ●

Editing Priorities
- ○
- ○
- ○
- ○
- ○
- ○

Other
_____
_____
_____
_____
_____
_____
_____

GOALS THIS WEEK

MONDAY

TUESDAY

WEDNESDAY

THURSDAY

FRIDAY

SATURDAY

SUNDAY

GOALS THIS WEEK

- MONDAY
- TUESDAY
- WEDNESDAY
- THURSDAY
- FRIDAY
- SATURDAY
- SUNDAY

GOALS THIS WEEK

MONDAY

TUESDAY

WEDNESDAY

THURSDAY

FRIDAY

SATURDAY

SUNDAY

GOALS THIS WEEK

- MONDAY
- TUESDAY
- WEDNESDAY
- THURSDAY
- FRIDAY
- SATURDAY
- SUNDAY

GOALS THIS WEEK

MONDAY

TUESDAY

WEDNESDAY

THURSDAY

FRIDAY

SATURDAY

SUNDAY

'Shiny' ideas this month

IDEA 1:

IDEA 2:

IDEA 3:

IDEA 4:

MONTHLY CHECK-IN

WHAT I ACHIEVED THIS MONTH

WEEK 1	WEEK 2	WEEK 3	WEEK 4

WEEK 5

STEPS TOWARDS GOALS

Notes:

July

MUST DO:

BE NICE IF:

July

1	2	3	4	5	6	7
8	9	10	11	12	13	14
15	16	17	18	19	20	21
22	23	24	25	26	27	28
29	30	31				

Writing Priorities
- ○
- ○
- ○
- ○
- ○
- ○

Marketing
- ●
- ●
- ●
- ●
- ●

Editing Priorities
- ○
- ○
- ○
- ○
- ○
- ○

Other
_____
_____
_____
_____
_____
_____
_____

GOALS THIS WEEK

MONDAY

TUESDAY

WEDNESDAY

THURSDAY

FRIDAY

SATURDAY

SUNDAY

GOALS THIS WEEK

- MONDAY
- TUESDAY
- WEDNESDAY
- THURSDAY
- FRIDAY
- SATURDAY
- SUNDAY

GOALS THIS WEEK

MONDAY

TUESDAY

WEDNESDAY

THURSDAY

FRIDAY

SATURDAY

SUNDAY

GOALS THIS WEEK

MONDAY

TUESDAY

WEDNESDAY

THURSDAY

FRIDAY

SATURDAY

SUNDAY

GOALS THIS WEEK

MONDAY

TUESDAY

WEDNESDAY

THURSDAY

FRIDAY

SATURDAY

SUNDAY

'Shiny' ideas this month

IDEA 1:

IDEA 2:

IDEA 3:

IDEA 4:

MONTHLY CHECK-IN

WHAT I ACHIEVED THIS MONTH

WEEK 1	WEEK 2	WEEK 3	WEEK 4

WEEK 5

STEPS TOWARDS GOALS

Notes:

August

MUST DO:

BE NICE IF:

August

1	2	3	4	5	6	7
8	9	10	11	12	13	14
15	16	17	18	19	20	21
22	23	24	25	26	27	28
29	30	31				

Writing Priorities
- ○
- ○
- ○
- ○
- ○
- ○
- ○

Marketing
- ●
- ●
- ●
- ●
- ●

Editing Priorities
- ○
- ○
- ○
- ○
- ○
- ○

Other
_____
_____
_____
_____
_____
_____
_____

GOALS THIS WEEK

MONDAY

TUESDAY

WEDNESDAY

THURSDAY

FRIDAY

SATURDAY

SUNDAY

GOALS THIS WEEK

MONDAY

TUESDAY

WEDNESDAY

THURSDAY

FRIDAY

SATURDAY

SUNDAY

GOALS THIS WEEK

MONDAY

TUESDAY

WEDNESDAY

THURSDAY

FRIDAY

SATURDAY

SUNDAY

GOALS THIS WEEK

- MONDAY
- TUESDAY
- WEDNESDAY
- THURSDAY
- FRIDAY
- SATURDAY
- SUNDAY

GOALS THIS WEEK

- MONDAY
- TUESDAY
- WEDNESDAY
- THURSDAY
- FRIDAY
- SATURDAY
- SUNDAY

'Shiny' ideas this month

IDEA 1:

IDEA 2:

IDEA 3:

IDEA 4:

MONTHLY CHECK-IN

WHAT I ACHIEVED THIS MONTH

WEEK 1	WEEK 2	WEEK 3	WEEK 4

WEEK 5

STEPS TOWARDS GOALS

Notes:

September

MUST DO:

BE NICE IF:

September

1	2	3	4	5	6	7
8	9	10	11	12	13	14
15	16	17	18	19	20	21
22	23	24	25	26	27	28
29	30					

Writing Priorities
- ○
- ○
- ○
- ○
- ○
- ○
- ○

Editing Priorities
- ○
- ○
- ○
- ○
- ○
- ○

Marketing
- ●
- ●
- ●
- ●
- ●

Other
_____
_____
_____
_____
_____
_____
_____

GOALS THIS WEEK

MONDAY

TUESDAY

WEDNESDAY

THURSDAY

FRIDAY

SATURDAY

SUNDAY

GOALS THIS WEEK

MONDAY

TUESDAY

WEDNESDAY

THURSDAY

FRIDAY

SATURDAY

SUNDAY

GOALS THIS WEEK

- MONDAY

- TUESDAY

- WEDNESDAY

- THURSDAY

- FRIDAY

- SATURDAY

- SUNDAY

GOALS THIS WEEK

MONDAY

TUESDAY

WEDNESDAY

THURSDAY

FRIDAY

SATURDAY

SUNDAY

'Shiny' ideas this month

IDEA 1:

IDEA 2:

IDEA 3:

IDEA 4:

MONTHLY CHECK-IN

WHAT I ACHIEVED THIS MONTH

WEEK 1	WEEK 2	WEEK 3	WEEK 4

WEEK 5

STEPS TOWARDS GOALS

Notes:

October

MUST DO:

BE NICE IF:

October

1	2	3	4	5	6	7
8	9	10	11	12	13	14
15	16	17	18	19	20	21
22	23	24	25	26	27	28
29	30	31				

Writing Priorities
- ○
- ○
- ○
- ○
- ○
- ○

Marketing
- ●
- ●
- ●
- ●
- ●

Editing Priorities
- ○
- ○
- ○
- ○
- ○
- ○

Other
_____
_____
_____
_____
_____
_____
_____

GOALS THIS WEEK

MONDAY

TUESDAY

WEDNESDAY

THURSDAY

FRIDAY

SATURDAY

SUNDAY

GOALS THIS WEEK

- MONDAY -

- TUESDAY -

- WEDNESDAY -

- THURSDAY -

- FRIDAY -

- SATURDAY -

- SUNDAY -

GOALS THIS WEEK

MONDAY

TUESDAY

WEDNESDAY

THURSDAY

FRIDAY

SATURDAY

SUNDAY

GOALS THIS WEEK

MONDAY

TUESDAY

WEDNESDAY

THURSDAY

FRIDAY

SATURDAY

SUNDAY

'Shiny' ideas this month

IDEA 1:

IDEA 2:

IDEA 3:

IDEA 4:

MONTHLY CHECK-IN

WHAT I ACHIEVED THIS MONTH

WEEK 1	WEEK 2	WEEK 3	WEEK 4

WEEK 5

STEPS TOWARDS GOALS

Notes:

November

MUST DO:

BE NICE IF:

November

1	2	3	4	5	6	7
8	9	10	11	12	13	14
15	16	17	18	19	20	21
22	23	24	25	26	27	28
29	30	31				

Writing Priorities
- ○
- ○
- ○
- ○
- ○
- ○
- ○

Marketing
- ●
- ●
- ●
- ●
- ●

Editing Priorities
- ○
- ○
- ○
- ○
- ○
- ○

Other
_____
_____
_____
_____
_____
_____
_____

GOALS THIS WEEK

MONDAY

TUESDAY

WEDNESDAY

THURSDAY

FRIDAY

SATURDAY

SUNDAY

GOALS THIS WEEK

MONDAY

TUESDAY

WEDNESDAY

THURSDAY

FRIDAY

SATURDAY

SUNDAY

GOALS THIS WEEK

MONDAY

TUESDAY

WEDNESDAY

THURSDAY

FRIDAY

SATURDAY

SUNDAY

GOALS THIS WEEK

MONDAY

TUESDAY

WEDNESDAY

THURSDAY

FRIDAY

SATURDAY

SUNDAY

GOALS THIS WEEK

MONDAY

TUESDAY

WEDNESDAY

THURSDAY

FRIDAY

SATURDAY

SUNDAY

'Shiny' ideas this month

IDEA 1:

IDEA 2:

IDEA 3:

IDEA 4:

MONTHLY CHECK-IN

WHAT I ACHIEVED THIS MONTH

WEEK 1	WEEK 2	WEEK 3	WEEK 4

WEEK 5

STEPS TOWARDS GOALS

Notes:
_____
_____
_____
_____

December

MUST DO:

BE NICE IF:

December

1	2	3	4	5	6	7
8	9	10	11	12	13	14
15	16	17	18	19	20	21
22	23	24	25	26	27	28
29	30	31				

Writing Priorities
- ○
- ○
- ○
- ○
- ○
- ○

Marketing
- ●
- ●
- ●
- ●
- ●

Editing Priorities
- ○
- ○
- ○
- ○
- ○
- ○

Other
_____
_____
_____
_____
_____
_____
_____

GOALS THIS WEEK

MONDAY

TUESDAY

WEDNESDAY

THURSDAY

FRIDAY

SATURDAY

SUNDAY

GOALS THIS WEEK

MONDAY

TUESDAY

WEDNESDAY

THURSDAY

FRIDAY

SATURDAY

SUNDAY

GOALS THIS WEEK

MONDAY

TUESDAY

WEDNESDAY

THURSDAY

FRIDAY

SATURDAY

SUNDAY

GOALS THIS WEEK

- MONDAY
- TUESDAY
- WEDNESDAY
- THURSDAY
- FRIDAY
- SATURDAY
- SUNDAY

GOALS THIS WEEK

MONDAY

TUESDAY

WEDNESDAY

THURSDAY

FRIDAY

SATURDAY

SUNDAY

'Shiny' ideas this month

IDEA 1:

IDEA 2:

IDEA 3:

IDEA 4:

MONTHLY CHECK-IN

WHAT I ACHIEVED THIS MONTH

WEEK 1	WEEK 2	WEEK 3	WEEK 4

WEEK 5

STEPS TOWARDS GOALS

Notes:

End of Year Reflection

TOP 5 ACCOMPLISHMENTS

-
-
-
-
-

PROJECTS COMPLETED

WHAT NEEDS MORE TIME

SURPRISES

GRATEFUL FOR

CHALLENGES I OVERCAME

NEXT STEPS

To order for next year,
please go to:
www.alyssacurtayne.com

www.ingramcontent.com/pod-product-compliance
Lightning Source LLC
Chambersburg PA
CBHW041713290426
44109CB00029B/2860